Gardens

All Kinds of
Gardens

by Mari Schuh

Consulting Editor: Gail Saunders-Smith, PhD

Content Consultant: Sarah Pounders
Education Specialist, National Gardening Association

CAPSTONE PRESS
a capstone imprint

Pebble Books are published by Capstone Press,
151 Good Counsel Drive, P.O. Box 669, Mankato, Minnesota 56002.
www.capstonepress.com

Printed in the United States of America in North Mankato, Minnesota
092009
005618CGS10

 Books published by Capstone Press are manufactured with paper
containing at least 10 percent post-consumer waste.

Library of Congress Cataloging-in-Publication Data
Schuh, Mari C., 1975–
    All kinds of gardens / by Mari Schuh.
    p. cm. — (Pebble books. Gardens)
    Summary: "Simple text and photographs present many kinds of
gardens" — Provided by publisher.
    Includes bibliographical references and index.
    ISBN 978-1-4296-3981-1 (library binding)
    ISBN 978-1-4296-4840-0 (paperback)
    1. Gardens — Juvenile literature. 2. Gardening — Juvenile literature. I. Title.
II. Series: Pebble (Mankato, Minn). Gardens.
SB457.S375 2010
635 — dc22   2009025588

Note to Parents and Teachers

The Gardens set supports national science standards related to life
science. This book describes and illustrates different kinds of gardens. The
images support early readers in understanding the text. The repetition
of words and phrases helps early readers learn new words. This book
also introduces early readers to subject-specific vocabulary words, which
are defined in the Glossary section. Early readers may need assistance to
read some words and to use the Table of Contents, Glossary, Read More,
Internet Sites, and Index sections of the book.

The author dedicates this book to Fran and Rebecca Carr of Omaha, Nebraska.

Table of Contents

All Kinds of Gardens

Gardens come
in all shapes and sizes.
Let's look at different gardens
to see what's growing.

Flowers and Vegetables

Beds of colorful blossoms bloom in a flower garden.

Beets and other vegetables
grow in rows
in a vegetable garden.

Wildlife Gardens

Wildlife gardens
have flowers, bushes,
and wild grasses.
These native plants
are easy to grow.

Wild animals use
wildlife gardens.
They eat, drink,
and rest in the shade.

Other Gardens

Container gardens aren't grown in the ground. These gardens grow in pots.

Plants in rock gardens
need just a little soil
to grow.

Water lilies float
in water gardens.
Koi fish swim
among the stems.

What kind of garden
will you grow?

Glossary

bed — a place in a garden where flowers are planted

bloom — to grow flowers

blossom — a flower on a plant

bush — a large plant with many branches

koi — a bright-colored fish that often lives in ponds

native — a plant or animal that originally lived or grew in a certain place

soil — the top layer of earth where plants can grow

stem — the long main part of a plant from which the leaves and flowers grow

Read More

Bodach , Vijaya Khisty. *Seeds.* Plant Parts. Mankato, Minn.: Capstone Press, 2007.

Krezel, Cindy. *Kids' Container Gardening: Year-Round Projects for Inside and Out.* Batavia, Ill.: Ball Publishing, 2005.

Schuh, Mari. *Growing a Garden.* Gardens. Mankato, Minn.: Capstone Press, 2010.

Internet Sites

FactHound offers a safe, fun way to find Internet sites related to this book. All of the sites on FactHound have been researched by our staff.

Here's all you do:

Visit *www.facthound.com*

FactHound will fetch the best sites for you!

Index

Word Count: 106
Grade: 1
Early-Intervention Level: 13

Editorial Credits
Jenny Marks, editor; Heidi Thompson, designer; Marcie Spence, media
    researcher; Eric Manske, production specialist; Sarah Schuette, photo stylist;
    Marcy Morin, scheduler

Photo Credits
Shutterstock/Ken Brown, 12
All other photos by Capstone Studio/Karon Dubke